Contents

Shopping around the world

All around the world, people shop.

Our Global Co

Shopping

Cassie Mayer

www.heinemann.co.uk/library
Visit our website to find out more information about Heinemann Library books.

To order:
☎ Phone 44 (0) 1865 888066
🖹 Send a fax to 44 (0) 1865 314091
🖥 Visit the Heinemann Bookshop at www.heinemann.co.uk/library to browse our catalogue and order online.

First published in Great Britain by Heinemann Library, Halley Court, Jordan Hill, Oxford OX2 8EJ, part of Harcourt Education. Heinemann is a registered trademark of Harcourt Education Ltd.

© Harcourt Education Ltd 2007
First published in paperback in 2008
The moral right of the proprietor has been asserted.

Editorial: Diyan Leake
Design: Joanna Hinton-Malivoire
Picture research: Ruth Smith
Production: Duncan Gilbert

Origination: Chroma Graphics (Overseas) Pte Ltd
Printed and bound in China by South China Printing Company Ltd

ISBN 978 0 431 19107 2 (hardback)
11 10 09 08 07
10 9 8 7 6 5 4 3 2 1

ISBN 978 0 431 19116 4 (paperback)
12 11 10 09 08
10 9 8 7 6 5 4 3 2 1

British Library Cataloguing in Publication Data
Mayer, Cassie
  Shopping - (Our global community)
  1. Fairs - Juvenile literature
  I. Title
  381.1'8

Acknowledgements
The publishers would like to thank the following for permission to reproduce photographs: Alamy Images pp. **11** (Charles Bowman), **12** (David R. Frazier Photolibrary, Inc), **16** (Greenshoots Communications), **18** (Glen Allison), **23** (Charles Bowman); Corbis pp. **4** (Michael S. Lewis), **6** (Frans Lemmens/ zefa), **7** (Barry Lewis), **8** (Bob Rowan; Progressive Image), **9** (Kevin Fleming), **10** (Jon Hicks), **13** (Michael Prince), **14** (Owen Franken), **15** (Hubert Stadler), **17** (Owen Franken), **19** (Dung Vo Trung), **20** (Tibor Bognár), **21** (Bob Krist), **22** (Barry Lewis), **23** (Michael S. Lewis; Barry Lewis); Getty Images pp. **5** (Stone).

Cover photograph of Chichicastanango Market, Guatemala reproduced with permission of Corbis/Tibor Bognar.

Every effort has been made to contact copyright holders of any material reproduced in this book. Any omissions will be rectified in subsequent printings if notice is given to the publishers.

People shop at markets.

spices

People sell things at markets.

stall holder

People shop with money.

Types of market

People shop in big supermarkets.

People shop in small farmers' markets.

Some markets are outside.

Some markets are inside.

What people shop for

People shop for fish.

People shop for meat.

People shop for bread.

People shop for cheese.

People shop for clothes.

People shop for toys.

Special markets

Some markets are on water.

Some markets are open at night.

All around the world, shopping
is different.

But all people need to shop.

Shopping vocabulary

stall holder

buyer

Picture glossary

 **inside** in a building

 **market** place where you can buy things

 **stall holder** person who sells things in a market

Index

Notes for parents and teachers

Before reading

Talk about shopping. Where do the children's families buy fruit and vegetables? Do they ever shop in a market? Talk about the differences between a shopping centre and a market.

After reading

Drama. Let four children be stall holders. They should decide what they are selling. The remaining children should be buyers at the market. Encourage the sellers to sell their wares – for example, by calling out, "Lovely fresh tomatoes! Bargains for everyone! Best value around!" Talk about bartering and agreeing a sale.

Rhyme. Make up verses for the rhyme: "To market, to market, to buy a fat pig / Home again, home again, jiggedy jig". Tell the children that the rhyming words do not need to be real words but they must rhyme – for example, "to buy a fat goat ... sliggedy sloat!"

Play "Granny went to market". Each child takes it in turn to add an item to the list of shopping but they must remember all the things that the other children have said.